Not For Long

By Angel D. Washington

Published by Angel's Diary © 2014
Photos by: Amber D. Armogan
ISBN: 978-0-9860041-2-4
Library of Congress Control Number: 2014932603

All rights reserved. No part of this book may be reproduced in any form or by any means without the prior consent of the Publisher, except brief quotes used in reviews. This is a work of fiction. Any references or similarities to actual events, real people, living or dead, or to real locales are intended to give the novel a sense of reality. Any similarity in other names, characters, places, and incidents is entirely coincidental.

~Dedication~

~Unbeknownst to many, they've personally offered inspiration…
In return, I offer my personal dedication~

~Always Inspired~
Angel D. Washington

~Preface~

Life is a journey that is full of challenges and triumphs that will ultimately define who we are as individuals. We all respond differently, which is indicative of the vast differences in us, as people. When faced with different situations, how do you respond? So I ask…

What If?

What if…
I wrote a book about you, what would the title be?
Would it suggest that you are a great leader, with a remarkable legacy?
A person that will leave your first class mark on this world…
That has touched the hearts and souls of every boy and girl?
Or would the title imply that you can never be trusted
Ready to betray the very moment, with confidence, you're entrusted?
Who. Are. You.?

Ask yourself, what if…
I wrote a book about you, what character would you play,
The villainous person with anger in your heart and misery to repay?
The cold hearted person that causes heartache and drama
That is always looking over their shoulder for that inevitable karma?
Or the person that has a beautiful soul and carefree spirit

That realizes that life is a blessing, so in peace and joy,
you live it???
Who. Are. You?

Because, what if…
I wrote a book about you, what story would be told?
About the life you live, honest and true or callous and cold?
Would the storyline be aligned with a gracious, spiritual being
That prides yourself on love, honor and the joy that you bring?
Or perhaps a plot about a ruthless, diabolical character of whom
Gets gratification as the happiness of others is personally consumed…
Who. Are. You.?

Seriously, what if…
I wrote a book about you, what would the many chapters tell?
About the person that you are, that readers would get to know so well?
Are you untrustworthy, dishonest, full of lies and deceit?
Without concern or care for the people that you mistreat??
Or do you live life with dignity, delight and self respect
Lovingly, wholeheartedly giving the world your absolute best??
Who. Are. You.?

I ask, 'cause, what if…
I wrote a book about you, what would the ending be?
Would it tell about a person that is living their dreams?
A person that works hard toward their aspirations without pause…
That you appreciate where you've been and the person that you are?
Or are you smug, vindictive and malicious within
That your reign of terror has a beginning, but has no end???
Who. Are. You.?

~Content~

BLISS

Lovers, Lies and Lullablies	11
You are Heaven on my Mother Earth	12
You Don't Know Me	13
Goodnight, My Love	14
Break The Code	15
Khaotic for Khat	16

BLUES

Not for Long	19
Your Eyes are Wide Shut	21
Widow	24
Superwoman	27

BEAUTY

The Beauty of It Is	30
Beautiful Complexity	31
Love Is	32
Aint Nun	34

BETRAYAL

Have You Ever Wondered?	36
Eclipse	38
Take A Number	40
Reality Is ...	42

BLESSINGS

Expecting	47
I'm So Thankful	48
Journey of Healing	49
I Stand Tall	50
Nobody Knows?	52
Your Ambition is their Competition	53

PERFORMANCE

Swag	55
Please Don't Kill My Dreams	58
Because I Loved You	60
A Brotha's Pain	61
My Poetic Soul	71

"Misery loves company, but Not For Long,
Because along comes..."
~Bliss~

LOVERS, LIES AND LULLABIES

Loving you being my lover
I promise and I tell you no lies
Emotionally and seductively in sync
Our bodies sing lullabies
With great intensity and passion
There is a volcanic eruption
Exhilarating, spine-tingling and gripping
Stimulating, mind blowing seduction
I love that you are my lover
I'm forthcoming, I tell you no lies
Magically and pleasurably in tune
Our bodies sing lullabies
Effortless emotion and fluidity
A smoothness between us two
Synchronized, two bodied symphony
Composed by me and you
I desire no other to be my lover
Pure honesty, I tell you no lies
We are the perfect lyrics to our song
Our bodies sing lullabies…

YOU ARE HEAVEN ON MY MOTHER EARTH

The aroma of your masculinity allows me the insight to God's Love
The feel of your touch caresses me so ~ and I can never get enough
Your body exudes such sexiness~ I dream with my eyes open
The sound of your voice, even in a whisper, is seductive, passionate and golden

In my eyes, you are perfection, my love
No jewel matches your worth
No matter the flaw, it's part of you
You are Heaven~
On my Mother Earth

When you part your lips to speak, I melt before a word is ever spoken
The chivalry that is embedded in your actions lets me know that I was chosen
Your embrace is protective, yet so gentle, I feel so safe in your grasp
You're my knight in shining armor, my love, for more, I could never ask

In my eyes, you are perfection, my love
No jewel matches your worth
No matter the flaw, it's part of you
You are Heaven~
On my Mother Earth

You are Heaven… On my Mother Earth

YOU DON'T KNOW ME

I remember the night that we met, not so long ago
You approached me, as I walked in the other direction
You knew what you wanted, you asked and I said no…
(playing hard to get)
Persistent and consistent, your desire was me
For this weekend, I could offer contentment and commitment
For such a short time, you and I would become, We
(glad you caught me)

You don't know me, I don't know you
You don't know me, secret rendezvous…
You don't know me, I don't know you
You don't know me, like you think you do…

A love affair so in touch with a dream, took us both by surprise
Spending every moment of two days together
By candlelight, staring into each other's eyes
(with a glass of wine)
It's so good, too good, we know, to be true, between us two
When our whirlwind love affair ended, my heart stopped
But reality is, you don't know me, and my Love,
(I don't know you)

Those moments that we shared
Will last forever
I wonder if you, too
Reminisce about our Secret Rendezvous
Even though you don't know me and I don't know you

Angel D. Washington

GOOD NIGHT, MY LOVE

Wait a minute, Sweetheart
Before you go to sleep
There's something that I want to say
For your soul to keep
My love for you is like a whisper
In the blizzard of a wind
My heart is reaching out to you
As the day begins
I fell in love overnight
And it wasn't hard to do
Especially when I felt the love
That came directly from you
Now is the time to say thank you
And finally say good night
I love you and thank you
Sleep well, now close your eyes
Good night, my Love, Good night

BREAK THE CODE

Mentally, can you break the code
Really stimulate my mind
Give it to me good in conversation
Allow me to verbally unwind
Emotionally, can you sit where I sit
Just for a little while
Allow yourself the vulnerability
In my stilettos, walk a mile
Spiritually, fuel my ferocious flame
With words of encouragement
Let my soul feel the depth of you
And feed off your nourishment
Psychologically, massage my thoughts
With morally respectable intent
I safeguarded my heart long ago
The proper mechanisms of defense
Prayerfully, can you break the code
With you, may I share my faith
Spiritually, how do you fare
Are we in a common place
Physically, refrain from touching my body
Mentally touch my mind
Penetrate my mind and inner thoughts
As though it was by design
Mentally, emotionally and spiritually
I welcome this experience to unfold
By allowing you to stimulate my mind
But can you break the code?

Angel D. Washington

KHAOTIC FOR KHAT

The Gentlemen go wild
 Freaky style
Will flash a golden smile
Dig through their secret file
To find that number to dial
Going through withdrawals
Cause it's been a while
 Minds have been lost
From the highest fee to no cost
Just call it boss
Cause they gotta have it.
It walks, it talks
Hell, it has no faults
 It's man's best friend
It keeps quiet when told
Keeps a brotha warm when cold
Makes him feel like gold
Can make a middle aged man feel young, not old
Keeps a Brotha on his toes
Keeps him company as the day unfolds
Would never confiscate the remote control
Watches the Orange, Rose and Super Bowl
Ladies, don't Y'all know
What I'm talking about
That thang that the fellas
 Can't seem to live without
It's at home, church, the club and at work
It's at the grocery store in the produce section
It comes in all shapes, sizes and colors
And makes for easy detection

Not For Long

Sistah's, it's chaos
The control that we've been given
Got' em slippin', flippin', trippin' out
 Always dippin' swearin' they pimpin'
Friend got'em tippin' into the house
Lyin' talkin' 'bout he was chillin' with his boys
And that's why he was late
Brothaman can't even think straight
Ladies, friend got'em mesmerized
Tellin' lies
Can't look you in the eye
Like Johnny Gill singing my, my, my, my, my, my, my
Ya shol' look good tonight
Got'em leavin' home in the middle of the night
Runnin' red lights
Just to stick it
There is an addiction with it
From the moment they get it
They don't care about color, they just have to hit it
Eenie Meenie Minie Mo' ~ they don't care how they pick it
Don't know where it's been, but will put their face all up in it
Will beg, plead, get on their knees if we'd just trick it
This description, Ladies, most Brotha's will fit it
Sistahfriends, Diva's
You must understand the power that we have
Cause, with us, Sistahs, is where it's at
Brothas ain't KooKoo for Cocoa Puffs
Brothas are Khaotic for Kat

"Troubling to the spirit, but Not For Long..."
~Blues~

NOT FOR LONG

You will…
Never Forget Losing… me
Especially when the memories replay
And I will…
Never Forget Losing… myself
When I convinced myself to stay
I know
Nothing Feels Like… what
I once felt when I was with you
But you
Never Felt Like
There was a job you needed to do
Easily I …
Nearly Forgot Love
As you selfishly deprived
You would…
Negate Family Liability
Fulfilling your selfish ego and pride
Really, I…
Never Failed Love
Because I'd never had it true
But you're
Not Fooling Love
Afraid of it, overcoming you
I am
Nobody's Fool Love
But you just failed to see
I would
Never Forsake Love
That I believed was meant to be

Angel D. Washington

Loveless you?
Null Foolish Love
Who never knew Loyalty…
Loveless me?
Not For Long
It will find me authentically…

YOUR EYES ARE WIDE SHUT

In this love thing, hand in hand, we were to stand side by side
And as MY man, in support of you, I graciously stood behind
As I uplifted you in life and spirit, I fully respected your grind
After a long days work, I massaged your shoulders and EGO to help you unwind
But you chose to overlook and take for granted a love so refined
Even with every hint that you gave, I didn't realize they were signs
Down for us, I was ride or die, a better woman, you won't ever find
With my pride and self-respect, I'm leaving and I'll remain dignified

Your eyes are WIDE shut and your selfishness, without a doubt has left you blind
And because of your darkness, my light has dimmed and it struggles to shine
I don't know the hour on the clock, but what I do know is that it's time
I refuse to carry your baggage, so the bags I've packed are mine…

With standing applause, I traveled your world in awe and admiration
As your woman, I was wholeheartedly in support of your dedication

A true testament of strength and leadership, I had every indication
That hand in hand, you and I would reach our final destination
The epitome, so I thought, of the leading man, yet, I had a revelation
That what I believed to be the perfect imagery was misrepresentation
You and your LACK of communication and deceitful characterization
Led to the harsh acknowledgment of my misinterpretation...

Your eyes are WIDE shut and your selfishness without a doubt has left you blind
And because of your darkness my light has dimmed and it struggles to shine
I don't know the hour on the clock, but what I do know is that it's time
I refuse to carry your baggage, so the bags I've packed are mine

Am I bitter, hell yeah, because I was bamboozled and Lord knows I was misled
Am I disgusted, absolutely, because I believed every word that you said
Am I disheartened, extremely, please trust there's proof in every tear that I shed
Without clarity for too doggone long, therefore, I must clear my head
Replaying your empty promises that for years I was force fed
On your shallow waters that appeared to have depth, for many years, I tread

Healing the break in my heart and soul, I will start there instead
The process begins tonight, when I lay ALONE in that king sized bed

Your eyes are WIDE shut and your selfishness without a doubt has left you blind
And because of your darkness my light has dimmed and it struggles to shine
I don't know the hour on the clock, but what I do know is that it's time
I refuse to carry your baggage, so the bags I've packed are mine
The moment has come for goodbye…

Angel D. Washington

WIDOW

Today, I'm a widow
Widowed from the force of the blow
Widowed from the words that were killing me slow
Widowed from the inevitable death of my soul
Widowed from the day, of my mind you took control
Today I'm a widow…
The promises that you made to me before we wed
My intuition told me different, but I believed you instead
So many nights, I'd lie awake in bed
Remembering every horrible thing that you said
The times when you would go upside my head
Your hurtful words and physical rage, I would dread
To be mistreated
I was so defeated
My self-worth, self pride, so depleted…
I'd ask myself, why???
How does one explain why they choose to abuse
Batter and bruise
Mentally subdue
Destroy and consume
The life of the person whom
They claim to love????
Often, I'd ask myself how
Could I continue on this road that leads to nowhere?
Frightened and scared
Leave you? I wouldn't dare…
I believed that in the depths of your soul, you cared
The same dreams, we shared
To fulfill those dreams without you… the thought, I couldn't bear…

Not For Long

That was the way my mind worked,
I was delusional...
Back then...
As they say, hindsight is 20/20
How true that is, today I see so clearly
Although you claimed to love me dearly
The daily anticipation of your mood, I was leery
Daily, weekly, monthly and yearly
I was abused, mentally, emotionally and physically...
I couldn't tolerate it any more...
Therefore,
Today, I'm a widow
Widowed from the force of the blow
Widowed from the words that were killing me slow
Widowed from the inevitable death of my soul
Widowed from the day of my mind, you took control
Today I'm a widow...
When I considered all of the things that I could do
All of the methods that I could use
All of the painful ways from which to choose
To.
Hurt.
You.
Aim and fire, not one time, but two?
Take a bat to that head of yours until you were black and blue?
Make a hot pot of grits and slowly pour them all over you?
As tempting as every option was...
It would make me just as bad as you...
So, I decided to let GOD handle you...
And I left.
I left you alive and alone.
I left you- to find my soul.

And I found it and it found me.
That was the day that I was set free.
You and your mental, physical and emotional abuse
Are dead to me.
Today, I'm a widow
Widowed from the force of the blow
Widowed from the words that were killing me slow
Widowed from the inevitable death of my soul
Widowed from the day, of my mind you took control
I am a widow.
Because I found my soul and my soul found me…
After years of pain, anguish and agony
I have been set free.
I am a widow…
Because, you are dead to me.

SUPERWOMAN

There used to be a time when you and I would share
Wonderful moments, passionate kisses and bedtime prayer
Giving thanks for one another and the love that we felt
And in the comfort of each other's arms, our bodies would melt
But lately, it seems to me as though
Nothing that I do seems to satisfy you anymore
You come home and drop your crap at the door
And walk right past me like I don't matter anymore
From slaving over the stove and cooking your favorite meals
To cleaning up your spoiled boy tendencies and your messy ass spills
I launder your dirty draw(er)s and your funky socks
Bust out the Tide with Bleach and remove all of those spots
I know that it may seem hard for you to believe
That I'm responsible for your ass being zestfully clean
AND I give a lot, yet receive nothing in return
We are disconnected, but you don't seem to be concerned
I entertain your friends and your co-workers, too
And I put you to bed after I make good love to you
I'm your confidant; I listen to all that you have to say
I massage your body when you've had a bad day
I make sure that I laugh at your "interesting" jokes
I make sure that I spend time with your "interesting" folks

Even when I'm tired, I take the dogs for a walk
Yet you continue to look at me like our problems are my fault
Did you forget that we are in this relationship together
Some things must change, or things will never get better
What exactly have I done to deserve this treatment
Because I've only supported and loved you and that's no secret

I'm all burned out and I can't do this anymore
If you're in it, let's do this, if not, there's the door
I've been your support and in return, I deserve something
Otherwise, Lover boy, you will lose your Superwoman…

"Pain brings about the unsightly, but Not For Long, because of undeniable..."

~Beauty~

THE BEAUTY OF IT IS...

The beauty of it is...
That the love is within
Within you
Just love...
Self love
Self respect
Self tolerance and
 the desire to accept
You for who *You* are.
Self allegiance
Self esteem
Self confidence allowing
You to dream
And just believe...
Self commitment
Self truth
Just seek the love within you
Because the beauty of it is...
That the love has always been
Within...
YOU

BEAUTIFUL COMPLEXITY

She is beautifully complex
Remarkably genuine at best
But often times she leaves him perplexed
Uncertain about what she expects
But it's simple, because she's expressed
Love, truth and respect
That's it, that's all..

Undeniably
Unapologetically
Her beautiful complexity
Emotional honesty and transparency
Sporadic insecurities
That he doesn't understand
Difference between woman and man
Her desire for pure love, effortlessly
Endlessly and relentlessly
Unconditionally and authentically
 Unbelievable simplicity…

Yet, he remains perplexed
Though, she expressed what she expects
Love, truth and respect
That's it, that's all…
She is beautifully complex
In her beautiful complexities…
Difference between woman and man
Beautiful Complexities that he will never understand…

LOVE IS~

Love is ~
The common denominator between us
In our lives in which we live

Peace is ~
The contentment in our hearts when we
Remember that Jesus forgives

Hope is ~
The spirit of belief and optimism
That we have in all mankind

Faith is ~
The loyalty in our Heavenly Father
No other is more divine

Truth is ~
The reflection that is all we see
As we look at ourselves in the mirror

Honor is ~
The obligation that we carry with us
As our reflection becomes clearer

Joy is ~
That wonderful emotion that overwhelms us
For more reasons than one

Life is ~
Receiving that standing ovation
For an exemplary performance, well done

Wisdom is ~
The heart and soul of our elders
As they share a priceless story
Comfort is ~
Being cradled by the Grace of God
To Him, be all the Glory

The Beautiful things in life…
Live life with Love, Peace, Hope, Faith, Truth, Honor, Joy…
And you will gain wisdom…
As God offers His divine comfort.

AIN'T NUN

Ain't nun dope like her, ain't none smoked like her
She's flawless in her blackness and can't nun cope like her
Not nan can swang like her, not nan can sang like her
Flawless in her blackness and not nan can hang like her
Beautifully black
Symmetrically stacked
Intellectually, not easily matched
Brilliantly unblemished
Curvy in her thickness
Her blackness, a masterpiece, yet unfinished
Ain't nun dope like her, ain't none smoked like her
She's flawless in her blackness and can't nun cope like her
Not nan can swang like her, not nan can sang like her
Flawless in her blackness and not nan can hang like her…

*"Dismal to the inner being, but
Not For Long..."*

~Betrayal~

HAVE YOU EVER WONDERED?

Could this really be
Did I really love this dude more than I loved me?
His love was for real, or so I believed
He smothered me so much that I couldn't breathe
Yet, the mere thought of losing him, I couldn't conceive
My life without him, I could never perceive
Mentally, I was in a place and I just couldn't leave
He was toxic
Toxic like fumes
Atomic like boom
Killing me softly, like poison consumed
The drug in my system that selfishly loomed
Subconsciously enveloped in his polluted cocoon
Doomed
I was doomed
Emotionally spent
Mentally bent
He took advantage of my love to the fullest extent
He occupied space in me and didn't pay rent
He abused my spirit without my consent
To emotionally misuse me was his intent
Because it wasn't love
It was cruel and unusual hatred of himself
Yet, it was extremely dangerous for my health
Blissfully bankrupt, no richness, no wealth
My happiness was placed on the back shelf
Due to his lack of personal love for self
I laid it to rest
But I had to digress
Or my state of mind would continually stress
But nevertheless

I had to get out of this loveless, heartless emotional mess
Again, I digress...
Could this really be
Did I really love this dude more than I loved me?
I did, but now I'm emotionally free
To find the love that was meant especially for me...
Emotionally, spiritually, mentally free
Because above all others, I MUST love me...

Angel D. Washington

ECLIPSE

This shine is mine
Meant exclusively and specifically for me to provide...
Amongst others, I equally divide...
I spread my serenity thin, just like the blue skies

But, here you come with your eclipse
Ready to obscure with your bleak spirit that's dimly lit
What is the benefit?
Of the shadowy darkness within you that exists?
You and your feeble and pathetic eclipse
Come for me, consistently? Every time you will miss...
My advice to you would be, Chile...ya bes' flip your switch...
Turn on your light...

Your eclipse is not beautiful, it's sinister and pitiful
So typical and cynical
It's almost criminal
Yet...I guess it qualifies as biblical
Because God speaks of the sinful
But you better recognize, this is critical
My joy overflows regardless and is incredibly plentiful

So, I remind you
Please don't try to eclipse my light...

There's brightness that I bring and happiness that I sing

Not For Long

The joy is remarkably deep within my inner being
This shine is mine,
Meant exclusively and specifically for me to provide...
Amongst others, I equally divide...
I spread my serenity thin, just like the blue skies
Therefore, your eclipse will never steal my shine...

TAKE A NUMBER

You don't have to like me, I don't waste my time on you
Trust and believe I don't lose one ounce of slumber
It's not like you're the first hater that I've come across
So B*#@%, please, get in line and take a number
I'm honored that you spend so much time worrying about
What I have, how I'm living or what I do
Wondering how I paid for this, asking about how I got that
When you need to be worried about you
Because I exude happiness, you wonder about my relationship
Trust and believe my man and I are just fine
Misery loves company, but you won't bring me down
Work on your SHHH** and quit worrying about mine
Trying to price my whip on the information super-highway and
Price checking my house and land
On the real, you ain't gotta be sneaky about it
Since he paid for it, B*#@%, ask my man
All up in my pockets, with your nosy ass, wondering about
What kind of stacks that I'm sitting on
I swear sometimes I wish I had a magic wand because
I would tell your ass, poof, B*#@%, be gone
Don't mistake me for a fool, though, I know your ass is trifling
While you grinning all up in my face
I'm not gonna turn my back to you, wait for you to stab me
Then dig deep and slowly twist the blade

Not For Long

I see you in my hindsight, eye-balling, mad-dogging
I'm truly amused, it's comedy, boo
I hear you whispering, gossiping, SHHH** talking, name calling
You strengthen me, but you're stressing you
I use you as my stepping stone, that's what haters are good for
Your back has my footprint embedded
Envy ain't a good look, but you wear it well
That's real talk, you damn right, I said it
All you need to know about me is that I'm blessed and I know it
The rest is none of your concern
But it would behoove you to address your jealousy issues
There's a lesson or two you could learn
If there was an eleventh commandment, trust and believe
It would be Thou shalt not hateth
Meant especially for haters of the world like yourself
Who prove themselves to be the fakest
Now that I have put your ass on blast about being envious
And hateful of myself and others
Just do you, cause you will never be me and stop
Worrying about the business of another
You don't have to like me, I don't waste my time on you
No need to repeat myself, I didn't stutter
It's not like you're the first hater that I've come across
So B*#@%, please, get in line and take a number…

REALITY IS...

Reality is that...
You and I make
We or Us or Mr. & Mrs. So and So
But, if you EVER decide that you don't want to be a We or an Us
By all means, you are free to go...
Here's the thing that you should know
And if you don't know
Let me make it so
That it's clear...

Understand
I DO NOT want a PART-TIME man
Giving half-assed love and affection
As I sense rejection
Because you're neglecting
Me
There is nothing acceptable about infidelity
Trust and believe
I'd rather you leave...
So, if you EVER decide that you don't want to be a We or an Us
Cause you're looking in another direction
At a simple woman
With plenty of imperfections
Because she's half your age, she becomes your selection
To act out your foul indiscretions
Using no protection
Playing Russian Roulette
With deadly infections

As I sit and question
Myself
Wonder about my health
As I look at my reflection
Wondering if it's my complexion
Or my mid-section that you fell out of love with???
When all along it's your deception
That has me second guessing
Who I am?
When you're the one with the problems
And you and your manhood can't solve them...
So you decide to bring the hurt home?
See, that type of behavior, I can't condone...
Therefore, if... you EVER decide...that you don't want to be a We or an Us...
 Just go...
Please don't misunderstand me
I am the HONEY to your TEA
The SUGAR to your CANE
The CHOCOLATE to your DROP
And the ORANGE FLAVOR to your TANG
And I love being all of those things
For you, my Man...
But, again, I am a woman
A secure, loving, and dedicated woman
Who has to remain strong for our family
The one who will pick up the pieces if you decide to leave...

 Let's not cross that fine line...
The unspoken contract has been signed
The responsibilities are yours and mine
With marriage and children comes dedication and time
No child of mine will be left behind

Neither will I...
There are priorities that must be in place
Sacrifices that must be made
The selfless job that we do everyday
With or without complaint...

Those young and naive "girls", who have yet to become women
Know ABSOLUTELY NOTHING about
Responsibilities
Or properly raising a family...
But if that's what makes you happy
Do you, because I am going to do me

And for the things that you may suggest that I lack?
Very possible, very well may be a fact...
But, for a quick moment, let me take you to school
Remind you of that 80/20 rule
For being imperfect, I will not be ridiculed...
 So, again, I just ask one thing of you

If you ever decide that a morally, spiritually and emotionally bankrupt
Home wrecking skank is the direction in which you choose to go
And your road of travel is to become a philandering, scum of the earth, whoremonger
With the neighborhood ho...
You are free to go
AND my head will NOT hang low
So...
If you decide that you don't want to be a We or an Us

Not For Long

By all means
Go...
And with pleasure, I'll bid you goodbye...
Ciao, Adios, Farewell, Sayonara, Au revoir, Arrivederci...
Kick rocks...
Because, My Life??? It WON'T stop

"Shaken faith? Maybe, but Not For Long, because in life, comes..."

~Blessings~

EXPECTING

I never imagined the wave of emotion
The immeasurable amount of love
As my eyes settled upon the small screen
Seeing the first photo of my beloved
From a miniscule dot, you grew within
My protective layer, my womb
And as you develop, my heart fills with
More love than I thought it could consume
For many months, you and I would bond
A bond that only we'd share
As you'd grow, together, we would be
God's miraculously perfect pair
I imagine the mistakes that I will make
After your arrival into this life
I imagine the fights that we would have
When we wouldn't see eye to eye
My love for you supersedes my fear
Dear Child, it has from day one
Nevertheless, my joy filled heart
Awaits every experience to come
Until the day we meet, my love
Our hearts will beat together
To be forever connected after your arrival
And maturity, is my prayer
I never imagined the wave of emotion
The immeasurable amount of love
That I would feel after learning that
I was expecting you, my beloved…

I'M SO THANKFUL

I'm so grateful, because the Lord, my God
Is so able, you see
He is so worthy of my praise
Cause He delivered me
I'm so faithful to the Lord for
His eternal mercy
He shows me infinite favor
And I'm full, spiritually
I'm thankful to Him and His grace
Oh, how I love Thee
He gave His only begotten Son
Who died on the cross for me
Faithfully, with humility,
I fall to my knees
He bestows His love, mercifully
Eternally, gracefully, and spiritually, you see
My heavenly father lives within me
Thankfully, prayerfully, I surrender to Thee
Because it is He, who blesses me endlessly.

JOURNEY OF HEALING

I have been on a self healing journey
A personal path so divine
I have to search for my inner strength and love
Myself, I have to find
A spiritually sound and inspiring walk
That only I can take
In order for some much needed changes
That only I can make
MY personal rehabilitation is a
Conscious decision by me
I choose to no longer expose what I dislike
A full release of negativity
Life takes us through so many changes
This is another test
When I rise above my circumstances
I will peak at my best
I will conquer greatness and prosperity
There's not a bit of doubt
Failure to believe in me, myself and I
I simply refuse to allow
Freedom of my mind, body and spirit
Simply open to receive
The spiritual grace and peacefulness
That will encompass my inner being…

Angel D. Washington

I STAND TALL

Today, I stand so tall, I can reach the mountain top
Ain't got no time to look back, you better check your watch, tick tock
Like Usain Bolt, watch me get somewhere, do what it is that I do best
I've sharpened my skills without a doubt, I've become better than all the rest
Don't misconstrue what I'm telling you, I'd set sail across a lonely sea
But it was a journey that I needed to make, to find who USED to be me
I even sank to the bottom like the Titanic, the trials became my test
My spirit, sunken on the oceans floor, lost at sea, a treasure chest
One day I woke up and decided that the bottom was no place for me
My intelligence, desire for --prosperity and the treasure from the chest broke free
I emerged, I arose, my spirit and soul refreshed and prepared for victory
Cause, I'm no longer a victim of circumstance, I'm a Child of Destiny
I skillfully squared up with the challenge, like Mayweather, had to be quick wit it
If things ain't going right, please believe I'ma throw a Chris Angel trick in it
I'm about to score the winning shot, so get your court side seat and watch the game

I will do everything I set out to do and I'm about to be a household name
Today, I'm standing real tall, who's gonna stand by my side
You bes' get on the bus real quick, cause like Rosa Parks I'm about to ride
Life will be great, I'm setting my personal standards to fully represent
In the end I'll be amongst the top notch players, in the midst of my element…

NOBODY KNOWS?

The trials that you don't speak about
The tribulations that you withhold
You don't have to share with human kind
Because, believe me, God knows
You are weathering a turbulent storm
From every direction the wind blows
Chaotic and never-ending downpour
You face alone 'cause nobody knows
Your burdens weigh heavily on your spirit
Away, you pray the suffering goes
You are praying to the right source, my friend
Soon through the darkness, God shows
He hears every prayer and catches your tears
He allows the tribulations to unfold
Trust in Him, HE will not forsake you
For our Holy Father, He KNOWS…
Remain faithful, no matter how difficult
When the pain is deep within your soul
Because through the burden HE will shine through
The Almighty Father God, HE KNOWS…

YOUR AMBITION IS THEIR COMPETITION

There are those whose ambition is another's competition
Whose dreams and goals
Tend to create friends or foes
And there are those whose obsession
Is to prevent another's progression and succession
Let this be a lesson
Keep your mind on track
Don't allow another's ignorance to hold you back
Be a motivator, a goal creator, an educator, a dream maker
A chance taker
Avoid the negative energies
Of jealousy and envy
Ones negativity has the ability
To affect the self-esteem
Of one who has the capability to succeed
Your ambition is their competition
While they waste time on you and yours
You will have accomplished your goals
While they're still knocking on closed doors
A mind is a terrible thing to waste
In the land of your dreams you must earn your place
Though negativity you'll always face
Knowledge is the key
It simply takes you to believe
That it is your aspirations that you will achieve

Pieces written specifically for

~Performance~

SWAG

It was instilled in me, long ago, that I could achieve
Every goal, every aspiration, and every single dream
My swag is unequivocally and indisputably the key
To becoming the extraordinary man that I'm destined to be
By thoroughly educating my mind it's my personal guarantee
That I will soon reach that pinnacle no matter how tough it may seem
I'm gonna tell it like it is, ya'll, cause it's best told by me
You can attain anything as long as you believe...

I got my swag on lock, my collar, I pop, I am the epitome of smooth
I'm suited and booted, and I'm smelling good, I captivate any room
In addition to that, I'm an academic scholar and I'm at the top of my game
It's my personal guarantee that in a few years... you will know my name

Despite what people may think or what the stereotypes may suggest
I'm not an angry man who's depressed, distressed, or under any duress
And although I may be colorfully tatted up all over my chest
I stand tall as I say that I've never been handcuffed and placed under arrest

Angel D. Washington

Contrary to what some may think, there are no anger issues to suppress
So, let me take a minute or two to put all of the nonsense to rest
Because I say it's so, then it is so, I'm success at its best
I'm on a spiritual high and thankful, that I am abundantly blessed

I got my swag on lock, my collar, I pop, I am the epitome of smooth
I'm suited and booted, and I'm smelling good, I captivate any room
In addition to that, I'm an academic scholar and I'm at the top of my game
It's my personal guarantee that in a few years… you will know my name

I'm a scholar and I'm stuntin' on 'em, it's not difficult, you see
'Cause I got the Hollywood swag and I got the Brooklyn steez
When I'm in the presence of the Top Dog, I speak articulately
But when I'm chillin' with my boys, it's a must, that I do me
The power is in the ability to turn it on and off with ease
You gotta know when to be hot as fire, or cool like the breeze
There is a balance in life, you better recognize who to please
Starting with yourself by conquering what you set out to achieve

I got my swag on lock, my collar, I pop, I am the epitome of smooth
I'm suited and booted, and I'm smelling good, I captivate any room
In addition to that, I'm an academic scholar and I'm at the top of my game
It's my personal guarantee that in a few years… you will know my name

Society says that I'm not supposed to succeed, based on who I am
But society won't dictate my success, cause society doesn't give a damn
It was instilled in me, long ago, that I had to be a man
A man of substance, a man of promise, a man with a master plan
Keeping it one hundred, I go hard, respect is what I demand
So, I'd appreciate it if you keep it real, so that we both understand
Sharpening my intellect, stepping up my swag, I'm telling you firsthand
That undeniably, without a doubt, I'm about to be society's number one man…
I got my swag on lock, my collar, I pop, I am the epitome of smooth
I'm suited and booted, and I'm smelling good, I captivate any room
In addition to that, I'm an academic scholar and I'm at the top of my game
It's my personal guarantee that in a few years… you will know my name

Angel D. Washington

PLEASE DON'T KILL MY DREAMS

I dream of being an actress
But it's not as easy as it seems
When I grow up, I want to be President
Please don't kill my dreams
My Mommy doesn't watch the news
Neither does my dad
Because there's many bad things
That make them very sad
Sometimes it's not safe, at all
For me to play in the park
Sometimes it's very dangerous
To be out after dark
Little kids, like me...
Like me...
Like me...
Like me…
Little kids, like me...
Want to grow up to be big and strong
Little kids, like me
Want to dance to our favorite song
Little kids, like me
Don't ever want to be afraid
Little kids, like me
Want you to put down the guns, okay?
There are too many victims lost
To gun violence every year
Innocent people can't live their lives
Without living everyday in fear
I dream of attending college one day
Not as achievable as it seems

Not For Long

Because of the senseless crimes
Please don't kill my dreams...
Leaving families in agony
Loved ones lost tragically
Outrageous amount of casualties
Why can't we live happily
Affecting mankind drastically
Together, we can save humanity
Gun violence equals brutality
Please stop the gun violence mentality...
Please... Don't kill my dreams

BECAUSE I LOVED YOU
(Dedicated to Every Victim of DV Tragedies)

I stood tall, because I loved you
Never thought I'd lose it all, because I loved you
I gave you my all, because I loved you
And you took it all, because I loved you
It was never a fight, it was passion
Frustration led to tongue lashing
Commit to me, is all I was asking
Now the world knows, what I was masking
But in your love world, you locked me
Yet, of my motherhood, you robbed me
In the midst of my promise, you stopped me
In the pursuit of my dreams you blocked me
Because I loved you.
Because I loved you, it's clear, now
Because I loved you, no more fear, now
Because I loved you, no more tears, now
Because I loved you, no longer here, now
Because I loved you.
Because I loved you, no more me, now
Because I loved you, unfulfilled dreams, now
Because I loved you, I'm at peace, now
Because I loved you, I have wings, now
Because I loved you.
Because I loved you, too soon, but I'm free, now
Because I loved you, my hopes will never be, now
Because I loved you, my pain, all will see, now
Because I loved you, for me, they grieve, now
All because…
I loved you.

This performance piece was inspired by Ntozake Shange's Obie Award-winning play <u>For Colored Girls Who Have Considered Suicide When the Rainbow Is Enuf</u> and Tyler Perry's movie, For Colored Girls.

A BROTHA'S PAIN

Brotha 1 (Physical Mental Abuse)
I want to apologize for your pain
Like still waters, it runs dangerously deep
I look at my reflection in the mirror and I grimace at the sight
Cause I see the pain in me
The pain is in my eyes, deep within my soul,
There is pain in my feet
The heart wrenching pain, like you, within me
It runs dangerously deep
There is no excuse for the wrongs that I have done
How can I ever make them right
There is no explanation for the tears that I caused
All of those lonely nights
I heard your cry, although I never listened
You see, the problem is within me
It's spiritual warfare- a powerful battle engaged in my soul
That you just can't see
When I hit you and stomped you, with the boots on my feet, my Queen
That wasn't me
That was the bastard demon that had captured my soul

And we are at war, cause I want to be free
When I cursed you, demoralized you with the brutality of the tongue
That wasn't me
That was the diabolical spirit of who'd resided in my soul
I will break free from captivity
I couldn't love you, I hated everything about myself
I couldn't be the man that you needed me to be
The anger in me made me someone else
But I'm about to break free
I want to apologize for your pain, my Queen
Like still waters, it runs dangerously deep
I look at my reflection in the mirror and I grimace at the sight
Cause I see the pain in me
I'm at the mercy of your forgiveness, mother of my child
The humility is within me
Look past my indiscretions and the permanent scars
Free me from the indignity
The heart wrenching pain, like you, within me
It runs dangerously deep
I apologize from the depths of my soul,
Beautiful woman, I'm sorry, my Black Queen...

Brotha 2 (Rape)
The heart wrenching pain, like you, within me
It runs dangerously deep
I apologize from the depths of my soul,
Beautiful woman, I'm sorry, my Black Queen
For the immeasurable anguish when your innocence was taken
Causing unimaginable pain

Not For Long

No words can explain how I hurt inside knowing
How in one moment, your life changed
No one understands the agony I feel as I relive
What transpired that sinful night
Knowing that I took your innocence because of my selfishness
You saying no, really meant alright
How dare you say no to me, I was the big man on campus
That was my mentality
I asked myself, who does this woman she think she is
Trying to preserve her virginity
I heard you cry, I felt the dampness of your tears
As they stained your perfect face
But I could care less, you tried to deny me
And I was offended and outraged
When I victimized you with the brutality of my body
Queen, that wasn't me
That was the diabolical spirit of who'd resided in my soul
I will break free from captivity
I know the harm that I've done, now I'm ashamed
My actions, so cowardly
The person that took sexual advantage of you that night
Queen, that wasn't me
I look at my reflection in the mirror, I grimace at the sight
What a terrible sight to see
I'm at the mercy of your forgiveness, my Sistah, because
The humility is within me
Look past my indiscretions and the permanent scars
Free me from the indignity
The heart wrenching pain, like you, within me

It runs dangerously deep
I apologize from the depths of my soul,
Beautiful woman, I'm sorry, my Black Queen

Brotha 3 (Infidelity/Disease)
The heart wrenching pain, like you, within me
It runs dangerously deep
I apologize from the depths of my soul,
Beautiful woman, I'm sorry, my Black Queen
I was dishonest and I never gave a doggone about you
Nor obviously me
Never in a lifetime did I think I'd be apologizing for
All of my lies and deceit
An abundance of love and lust from many women
Is one man's dream
A different, yet beautiful woman every other night
Is a truly magnificent thing
I always felt, who were you to question where I was, what I was doing
Why and with whom
You were lucky enough that I took you as my bride
And I agreed to be your groom
In hindsight, I played Russian Roulette with my life, your life
I showed so little concern
Little did I know, that my indiscretions would burn me
Unfortunately, WE both got burned
You were my wife, yet I never carried you over the threshold
How selfish could I be
Yet I carried the virus over the threshold, into our home
Because of infidelity

Not For Long

My soul aches, my heart breaks for being the sole cause of
Your unimaginable grief
Your mental, physical health and well being in exchange
Allowing me to be a sexual thief
Can you, will you, Queen, find forgiveness in your heart
Especially for me
The man that you vowed to love, before GOD - til death do us part
Free me from humility
The heart wrenching pain, like you, within me
It runs dangerously deep
I apologize from the depths of my soul
Beautiful woman, I'm sorry, my Black Queen…

Brotha 4 (Mistreatment/Abandonment by Man)
The heart wrenching pain, like you, within me
It runs dangerously deep
I apologize from the depths of my soul,
Beautiful woman, I'm sorry, my Black Queen
I look at my reflection in the mirror, I grimace at the sight
Cause I see the pain in me
The pain is in my eyes, anguish in my spirit
An indescribable grief
There's no other way to justify my abandonment, when mentally
You weren't at your best
Selfishly, I left you when you were most susceptible to falling
Victim to yourself
I was empty inside, the pain wouldn't subside
What could I do for you

Leaving you to fend for yourself, to seek help on your own
I thought was best to do
I never imagined that you would contemplate suicide
When the rainbow was too much
I didn't recognize the signs of your sorrow, your grief
That life for you was so tough
I'm here now, woman, I've battled my issues
Never to abandon you again
I'm so sorry, Black woman, that when you needed me most
Without looking back, I ran
Only a dishonorable person would find peace in my actions
But I have forgiven myself
Now I stand before you, to ask for your forgiveness
Because, I too, needed help
You said that you found God in yourself and you love HER
I want to find HER in me
I'm told that SHE is a forgiving GOD, I know that SHE
Will forgive me totally
The heart wrenching pain, like you, within me
It runs dangerously deep
I apologize from the depths of my soul
Beautiful woman, I'm sorry, my Black Queen…

Brotha 5 (Slaying)
The heart wrenching pain, like you, within me
It runs dangerously deep
I apologize from the depths of my soul
Beautiful woman, I'm sorry, my Black Queen
That I took what was most important to you and me

Not For Long

As I stood before the window
I realized the pain that I caused for the both of us
As soon as I let go
With malicious intent, pure and authentic evil in my heart
I predicted your heartache
Then I became obsessed and mentally driven to see the tears
Permanently stain your face
I'm at war, with myself... at war with a demon
The hatred in me took its toll
I was enticed by the vision of your heart ache, your heart break
And it conquered my soul
But I'm sorry, so very sorry, I loved those children
Don't you see me on my knees?
GOD give them back to this beautiful woman to hold again
GOD I'm begging you, please!
There was a war going on in my head, beautiful woman
A battle that I couldn't win
I was serving on the front lines in my mind, in my soul
The sound of gunshots wouldn't end
My GOD, what have I done? Are they gone forever, GOD?
My GOD, forgive me for I have sinned!
Please give me back my babies, to love and to cherish
To hold in my arms again
The heart wrenching pain, like you, within me
It runs dangerously deep
I apologize from the depths of my soul
Beautiful woman, I'm sorry, my Black Queen...

Brotha 6 (Abortion)
The heart wrenching pain, like you, within me
It runs dangerously deep
I apologize from the depths of my soul
Beautiful woman, I'm sorry, my Black Queen
For taking advantage of an impressionable mind
Simply to benefit myself
For selfishly implanting your womb with my seed, not knowing
It would jeopardize your health
I didn't consider that you would handle the situation all on your own
In a low down, back alley clinic
Would I have listened or even cared about your personal problem
Not even for a minute
But that was who I was, no longer who I am, I've changed
I've matured, please understand
Your delicate life was in the balance and I'm sorry for my part
As an irresponsible young man
Good vs Bad is something that we all face on earth
There's the easy road or a path of trouble
In life, there are inner demons that we all must battle
It's a personal choice to win the struggle
My soul aches, my heart breaks for contributing to
Your inconceivable pain
Your mental, physical health and well being in exchange
For my personal and sexual gain
The heart wrenching pain, like you, within me
It runs dangerously deep
I apologize from the depths of my soul
Beautiful woman, I'm sorry, my Black Queen

Not For Long

Brotha's 1-6 (Collective)
Red with anger, is what my brother felt
When he battled the demon inside
An abusive man is not worthy of respect
When his arrogant deeds won't subside
Green with illness, mentally and physically
He doesn't recognize his own reflection
Staring directly into the eyes of death
Living life with a deadly infection
Blue with terror in his evil eyes
Morally bankrupt this man was
It's hard for you or I to understand
Immoral is as immoral does
Yellow with bitterness, my brother felt cheated
In life, he never found the good
So he wanted you to feel substandard, as well
Hurting you in every way he could
Orange with fury, whenever denied his wish
He would likely retaliate
A man that didn't even love himself
He was passionately filled with hate
Brown, yet empty, there was nothing inside
A heartless brother, that loved no one
Who suffered at the hands of man's war
Could the damage ever be undone???
Mothah's, Sistah's, Auntee's and Cousins
Some damages are a hard repair
Brotha's succumb to pain and hurt, too
Some, unable to deal with despair
We are sorry for the sorrow, the agony
That we sometimes put you through
For the physical, mental and emotional rollercoaster
And the eyes that are black and blue…

Angel D. Washington

The heart wrenching pain, like you, within me
It runs dangerously deep
I apologize from the depths of my soul,
Beautiful woman, I'm sorry, my Black Queen…

I write because it's in my spirit, it's in my soul.
So, I share the stories from the lives of many, yet in my words, from...

MY POETIC SOUL

It is my confession
That my true obsession
Is my poetic expression
Written in no specific direction
Or with any discretion
Yet it's a direct reflection
Of MY perception
In that, there is no correction
No misconception, no imperfections
About how I feel when I write
'Cause my poetic journey is MY lesson
My therapy session
That I choose to share with you
So listen up, here is my personal truth
When I articulate it, I'm sincere
When I speak it, you hear
When I read it, you cheer
When I type it, I'm clear
When I bring it, I fear
Myself, with every poetic word
I shed blood, sweat, and tears…
MY poetic flow, derives from my poetic soul
Sometimes I have no control
As my words take you on a poetic stroll
Of highs and lows
Dreams and goals
And those secret fantasies, of which no one knows

Angel D. Washington

My inner self, I expose
Willingly, I suppose
At war with myself, so anything goes
Yet, I have my truths to honor and uphold
And although I have a heart of gold
Occasionally my heart may seem cold
Because my approach may be bold
When poetically speaking in a poetic flow
For real though, my story is one to be told
So well written, perhaps it should be sold
Allowing a rhythmic story to unfold
From deep within my poetic soul.

www.ingramcontent.com/pod-product-compliance
Lightning Source LLC
Chambersburg PA
CBHW071413040426
42444CB00009B/2232